BEETLES

A TRUE BOOK®

by

Ann O. Squire

Ⲫ

Children's Press®
A Division of Scholastic Inc.

New York Toronto London Auckland Sydney
Mexico City New Delhi Hong Kong
Danbury, Connecticut

A harlequin beetle
takes flight.

Reading Consultant
Nanci R. Vargus, Ed.D.
Assistant Professor
Literacy Education
University of Indianapolis
Indianapolis, IN

Content Consultant
Jeff Hahn
Department of Entomology
University of Minnesota

Dedication:
For Evan

The photo on the cover shows
a gray ladybird beetle. The
photo on the title page shows
a may beetle.

Library of Congress Cataloging-in-Publication Data

Squire, Ann.
    Beetles / by Ann O. Squire
        p. cm. — (True books)
    Includes bibliographical references and index (p.)
    ISBN 0-516-22658-4 (lib. bdg.)   0-516-29358-3 (pbk.)
    1. Beetles—Juvenile literature. [1. Beetles]. I. Title. II. True book.
QL576.2 S67 2003
595.76—dc21

                                                        2002005883

CHILDREN'S PRESS, and A TRUE BOOK®, and associated logos are
trademarks and or registered trademarks of Scholastic Library Publishing.
SCHOLASTIC and associated logos are trademarks and or registered
trademarks of Scholastic Inc.

1 2 3 4 5 6 7 8 9 10 R 12 11 10 09 08 07 06 05 04 03

Contents

Although they look very different, ladybugs and fireflies are both beetles.

Meet the Beetles

Did you know that a ladybug is really a beetle? How about a firefly? Both of these insects, and many more, belong to the **order Coleoptera.** This order includes beetles as small as the head of a pin and as large as a rat. Beetles eat nearly every type of food and are found in every habitat on Earth, except salt water and the polar ice caps. Beetles are probably the most successful group of animals on Earth, with approximately 350,000 different species.

Despite their different habits and different sizes, all beetles share some common characteristics. Like other insects, beetles have bodies that are divided into three segments. They also have six

The exoskeleton is the tough outer shell that covers a beetle (above). A beetle's antennae help it to sense what is going on around it (right).

legs, hard outer shells called **exoskeletons,** and antennae that help them to find out about the world. But beetles have something that other insects don't have: a pair of tough, leathery forewings. These forewings work like suits of armor to protect the beetles' bodies and their delicate flight wings.

These hardened wings, called **elytra**, may be one of the keys to the beetle's incredible success. Protected by the elytra, a beetle can crawl around under leaves and debris. It can also

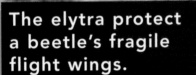

flight wings

elytra

The elytra protect
a beetle's fragile
flight wings.

squeeze into small crevices
where other insects might
damage their wings or be
squashed. When a beetle
wants to fly, it holds its elytra
up and out to the side and
then unfolds its flight wings.

Another thing that all beetles have in common is their mouthparts, which are designed for chewing. As you'll see in the next chapter, beetles eat all sorts of foods (including some things you probably don't think of as food), but all of them are things that can be chewed. Many beetles have large, dangerous-looking jaws called **mandibles** that they use to capture flies and other insects.

Some ground beetles feed only on snails, using their long, hooked mandibles to reach into the snail's shell and pull out the victim.

Champion Eaters

Beetles eat a truly amazing variety of food. In fact, almost everything in the world serves as food for some type of beetle. There are beetles that eat other insects; beetles that eat fish; beetles that eat dead animals; beetles that eat leaves, bark, or wood;

These rove beetles (top) are feeding on a dead cave cricket. A scarab beetle is chewing on a leaf (bottom).

and even beetles that eat dung! A beetle's choice of food can make it either popular or unpopular with humans. The ladybird beetle, or ladybug, is an insect that most people like. This beetle eats aphids, which are tiny, green insects that harm plants by sucking the juices out of them. Some gardeners buy ladybugs by the pound and release them in their flower beds to gobble up aphids.

Ladybugs eat many aphids each day.

Unfortunately, many other beetles are not as helpful. Wood-boring beetles can tunnel into the beams that hold up a house, while carpet beetles gnaw away at rugs,

Some beetles feed on grains, such as this dried pasta.

wool blankets, down jackets, and even stuffed animals. In the kitchen, grain beetles eat flour, dried pasta, and cereal. Out in the yard, cucumber beetles lunch on the cucumbers, cantaloupe, and squash in the vegetable garden. Bark beetles tunnel under the bark of trees to lay their eggs.

Most of these beetles are little more than a minor inconvenience. In fact, you probably wouldn't even know that most of them were there. But some beetles—and their very large appetites—are impossible to miss. The boll weevil, for example, is one of the most hated beetles,

A boll weevil can quickly destroy many cotton plants.

because it feeds on cotton plants. In the last hundred years, these tiny beetles have caused $14 billion dollars worth of damage to U.S. cotton crops.

Mating and Reproduction

When it's time to mate, the first thing a beetle needs to do is find a beetle of the opposite sex. Many female beetles advertise themselves with powerful chemicals. These chemicals are called pheromones, which are carried on the wind and attract males from far away. A few beetles use special sounds to attract mates, and some (fireflies and glowworms) send light signals to lure potential mates.

Fireflies use their light signals to attract mates.

Some beetles lay their eggs on the underside of leaves.

Once mating has occurred, female beetles lay their eggs, usually making sure there is food nearby. Some beetles lay their eggs inside fruit or seeds, on the underside of leaves, inside ant nests, or under the bark of trees. When the eggs hatch, the young beetles' favorite foods are ready and waiting.

Beetles go through many changes on their way to becoming adults in a process called **metamorphosis**. After hatching, the young beetles are known as **larvae**, and usually look nothing like the adults. Some are simple, wormlike creatures called grubs, while others are well developed. A larva's only job is to eat. During

this phase—which can last for as little as a week or as much as several years, depending on the type of beetle—the insect does little but eat and grow. As it grows its tough, outer skin becomes tighter and tighter. Soon the larva must shed its old skin. Most beetle larvae shed their skins three times, but some shed as many as fourteen times.

Eventually, the larva stops eating and moves to a sheltered spot underground or on a plant. Sometimes it spins a protective silken cocoon around itself. The insect is now called a **pupa**. Although it doesn't move around, big

This larva has wrapped itself in a cocoon for protection (right). This pupa looks very similar to an adult beetle (below).

changes are taking place, including the growth of wings and the development of eyes. When the changes are complete, the insect cuts its way out of the pupal case and begins the last phase of its life as an adult beetle. Amazingly, the adult phase is often the shortest part of a beetle's life cycle. Some adult beetles live for only one day before they die.

The World of Beetles

Scarab beetle

Scarab beetle

Beetles have lived on Earth for about 265 million years and are the largest single order of animals. In fact, one out of every three animal species is a type of beetle.

Cameroon beetle

Bright red beetle

Beetle Defenses

Beetles have many ways of protecting themselves against enemies. Their most basic protection is the hard, shell-like elytra. Some beetles are also covered with short, spiky hairs that make them even more distasteful to predators.

This South African beetle has short, spiky hairs on its body.

Ground beetles can easily
blend into their surroundings.

Many beetles hide from
their enemies by blending in
with their environments.

Ground beetles (which, as their name suggests, live on the ground) are dark colored and dull. Some weevils come in brilliant shades of green, which helps to conceal them as they feed on leaves. One of the most unusual camouflage artists is a hairy jewel beetle from Africa. This beetle is thought to gather yellow pollen on its black back so that it resembles the center of a flower.

This brightly colored
ladybug is hard to miss.

On the other hand, there are
beetles so brightly colored that
it's impossible to overlook
them. One of these is the
familiar red-and-black ladybug,
which would seem to be easy

prey as it rests on a leaf. When it is attacked, however, the ladybug emits a terrible-tasting yellow liquid that sends potential predators running.

Other beetles use even stronger poisons. Blister beetles actually have poisonous blood. When one of these

Blister beetles will bleed poisonous blood to escape an enemy.

beetles is handled, it begins to bleed, covering the attacker with a chemical that causes painful blisters to form. When a bombardier beetle is disturbed, it takes aim with its rear end and fires a boiling hot, explosive charge.

Tumbling flower beetles don't rely on their looks or on chemical weapons, but instead use quick, acrobatic movements to avoid being captured. The click beetle leaps into the air with a loud, snapping sound that surprises predators, and if the beetle is lucky, scares them away.

35

Some Amazing Beetles

Of all the beetles we've met so far, few are as amazing as the group known as dung beetles. Their favorite food is something we find disgusting: animal droppings! As soon as a cow, sheep, or other animal drops a dung pat, many different insects (including flies,

beetles, wasps, and more) begin to investigate it. The competition for fresh dung can be quite intense. Dung beetles have found a unique way to

37

A dung beetle rolls away its dung ball to eat later.

avoid competition. They break off a chunk of dung, form it into a ball, and roll it away, burying it safely underground to enjoy later. Female dung beetles lay their eggs inside dung balls—one egg per ball. When the egg hatches, the larva feasts on dung, eventually eating its way out of its cozy home.

Most beetles are found on dry land, but there are several unusual types that make the water their home. Diving beetles spend a lot of time underwater, where they prey on snails, other insects, tadpoles, and even small fish. These beetles have

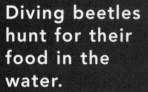
Diving beetles hunt for their food in the water.

solved the problem of getting oxygen while submerged by storing a small bubble of air underneath their elytra. This system works so well that diving beetles can stay underwater for up to several hours before they need to return to the surface for a new bubble of air.

Whirligig beetles also live in the water, but these insects are usually found on the surface, where they eat smaller insects that have fallen into the water. Because they stay on the surface, getting oxygen is not a problem. However,

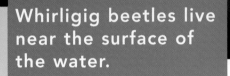

Whirligig beetles live near the surface of the water.

the water's surface is a dangerous place. Fish can attack from below and birds can swoop down from above. To deal with this kind of danger, you'd need two pairs of eyes—and that's just what the whirligig beetle has! Two eyes on the bottom of the head look straight down, and two on the top look straight up. What's also interesting is the upper eyes are specialized for seeing through air, and the lower eyes are specialized for seeing through water. With features like those, it's no wonder that beetles are the world's most successful animals.

To Find Out More

If you'd like to learn more about beetles, check out these additional resources.

 **Books**

Patent, Dorothy Hinshaw. **Beetles and How They Live.** New York, NY: Holiday House, 1978.

Organizations and Online Sites

Bug Bios
http://www.bugbios.com

A great Web site with close-up photos and descriptions of many different kinds of beetles (and other insects). Also includes links to a wide variety of insect sites and articles about insects in art, history, and culture.

Extreme Science
http://www. extremescience.com

Information on goliath beetles, plus lots of interesting facts on other types of insects.

Insecta Inspecta
www.insecta-inspecta.com/ beetles/scarab

An introduction to the behavior and history of scarab beetles.

Important Words

Coleoptera the scientific order of animals that includes beetles

elytra hardened wings that cover and protect a beetle's back and flight wings

exoskeleton the hard outer covering of an insect's body

larva an insect at its first stage of development after coming out of the egg and before becoming a pupa. Larvae are sometimes also called grubs.

mandible jaw

metamorphosis the complete change in form that insects go through as they develop

order a group of creatures within a class that shares certain characteristics

pupa the stage in an insect's life between the larval and adult stages

Index

Meet the Author

Ann O. Squire has a Ph.D. in animal behavior. Before becoming a writer, she spent several years studying African electric fish and the special signals they use to communicate with each other. Dr. Squire is the author of many books on animals and natural science topics, including *Seashells, Fossils, Animal Homes,* and *Animal Babies.* She lives with her children, Emma and Evan, in Katonah, New York.